I Like Giving.

THE 7 WAYS OF LIVING GENEROUSLY

Give, share, and show you care.

 GENEROUS THOUGHTS: Use a thought in my mind to think something kind.

 GENEROUS WORDS: Use what I say to make someone's day.

 **GENEROUS MONEY:** Use my money — no matter how much — if there is a life I can touch.

 GENEROUS TIME: Use any moment in my day to put Generosity on display.

 GENEROUS INFLUENCE: Use the choices that I make to affect the actions other people take.

 GENEROUS ATTENTION: Use my eyes to look and ears to hear. Listen well and distractions disappear.

 GENEROUS BELONGINGS: Use what I have to share — I can do this anywhere.

Koko the Kangaroo and the Big-Hearted Belongings

Copyright © 2024 by I Like Giving.®

Author Betta Tugive is the pen name for the I Like Giving.® Writing Team.

Scriptures taken from the Holy Bible, New International Version®, NIV®. Copyright © 1973, 1978, 1984, 2011 by Biblica, Inc.™ Used by permission of Zondervan. All rights reserved worldwide. www.zondervan.com. The "NIV" and "New International Version" are trademarks registered in the United States Patent and Trademark Office by Biblica, Inc.™

All rights reserved. No part of this book may be reproduced or transmitted in any form or by any means, electronic or mechanical, including photocopying and recording, or by information storage or retrieval system, without permission in writing from I Like Giving.®

Printed in the United States of America 2024.

ISBN 979-8-9897198-5-3

**Dedicated to Dave and Trish —
big-hearted givers.**

I Like Giving.® Writing Team:
S.F. Aughtmon
and friends

Illustrated by
Ben Cole & Andy Towler

Special thanks to Preston, Kayli, and Trevin

The Giving Adventure Series

**Jasper G and the
Me-Thinking Madness**

**Ellie the Elephant and the
Stinkin' Thinkin'**

**Polly the Parrot and the
Wonderful Words**

**Marco the Monkey and the
Marvelous Money**

**Stanley the Sloth and the
Tremendous Timekeeper**

**Leroy the Lion and the
Incredible Influence**

**Franny the Flamingo and the
Amazing Attention**

**Koko the Kangaroo and the
Big-Hearted Belongings**

KOKO THE KANGAROO
AND THE
BIG-HEARTED BELONGINGS

BY

Betta Tugive

I Like Giving. Publishing
Colorado Springs, CO

In the land of the givers where giving brings cheer, lived a fun kangaroo who collected sweet gear.

Koko loved all the stuff from her favorite team.

Power purple and green! They're my basketball dream.

The big Hoop-It-Up Tourney is starting today, and our team, Purple Lightning, has skills. **They can play.**

Marco knocked on her door.

"I am bringing this player, our number one guy! He can jump. He can shoot. He can steal. He can fly! It's my Kenny the King Alley-Oop figurine. He's the best power forward. You know what I mean?"

Here's a beanie. A jersey. A pair of green socks. Try them on. You can keep them. This warm-up suit rocks!

Marco started to grin.

"Koko, do you suppose that a monkey-sized me will fit into these clothes?

It'll work! These are stretchy.
We'll roll up the pants.
You can cinch up the waistband.
Just give it a chance.

Now I know that you love me.
I've known from the start.
And you've shown me you care
with your big-hearted heart.

But it still seems to me that we're not the same size.
And no matter the outfit or how many tries,
that's not going to change. I'll be fine. You will see.
Koko, you tried your best to share outfits with me.

Koko thought,

What a bummer. What else can I do?

How can Marco get in on our team spirit too?

Marco jumped.

And he flipped.

And he yelled out with joy.

**Koko, thanks!
You're the best.
I sure love this cool toy.**

With their big happy thoughts
and their hearts full of fun,
the pals cheered on their team.
And you guessed it — they won!

So now, what about you?
Have you been in that place?
Do you want to put smiles
on your special pal's face?

Feel the great thrill of giving — it just can't be bought!
And the real joy of sharing is something that's caught!

You see, giving to pals fills your heart to the top.
Share your Generous Belongings, and don't ever stop!

Talk About It & Put It Into Action!

How did Koko share with her pal Marco?

What are some creative ways you can share Generous Belongings with your friends?

Big-Hearted Challenge

As a family, come up with a list of people you know that would be blessed by a gift. Then, see if you have belongings in your home that fit the needs on your list, or would simply delight others. Experience the joy of sharing your belongings together and see how it sparks Generosity in others!

More To Explore In The Digital Portal!

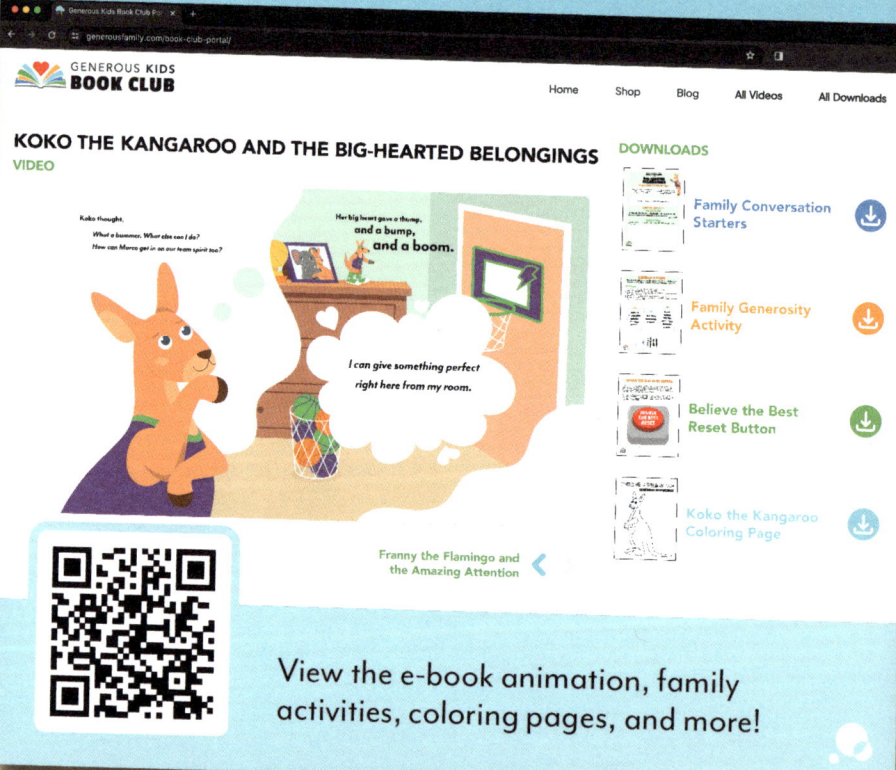

View the e-book animation, family activities, coloring pages, and more!

Anyone who has two shirts should share with the one who has none, and anyone who has food should do the same.
Luke 3:11 (NIV)

GENEROUS STUDENTS
HOMESCHOOL EDITION

Join the Generosity Road Trip! **Generous Students™: Homeschool Edition** explores The 7 Ways of Living Generously for all age groups!

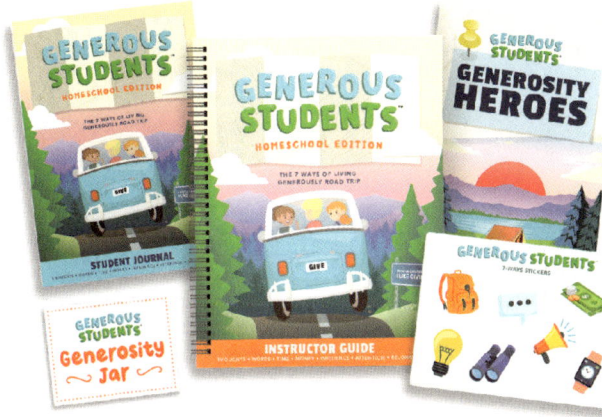

generousfamily.com

K-2

Check out our K-8 faith-based, biblical SEL curriculum! Generous Classroom™ is sharing the importance of gratitude and teaching the next generation how to be life-long givers!

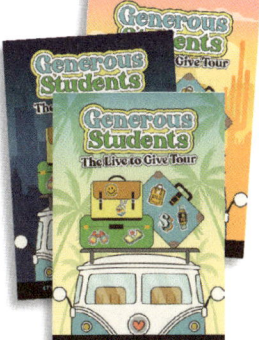
3-5

Middle School

generousclassroom.com